HAL•LEONARD
INSTRUMENTAL PLAY-ALONG

TENOR SAX

Disney Classics

THE CD IS PLAYABLE ON ANY CD PLAYER. FOR PC AND MAC USERS, THE CD IS ENHANCED SO YOU CAN ADJUST THE RECORDING TO ANY TEMPO WITHOUT CHANGING PITCH.

The following songs are the property of:
BOURNE CO.
Music Publishers
5 West 37th Street
New York, NY 10018

Baby Mine
Give a Little Whistle
Heigh-Ho
I've Got No Strings

Some Day My Prince Will Come
When You Wish Upon a Star
Whistle While You Work
Who's Afraid of the Big Bad Wolf?

Disney characters and artwork © Disney Enterprises, Inc.

ISBN 978-1-4584-1599-8

WALT DISNEY MUSIC COMPANY
WONDERLAND MUSIC COMPANY, INC.

DISTRIBUTED BY

7777 W. BLUEMOUND RD. P.O. BOX 13819 MILWAUKEE, WI 53213

Visit Hal Leonard Online at
www.halleonard.com

ALICE IN WONDERLAND
from Walt Disney's ALICE IN WONDERLAND

TENOR SAX

Words by BOB HILLIARD
Music by SAMMY FAIN

BABY MINE

from Walt Disney's DUMBO

TENOR SAX

Words by NED WASHINGTON
Music by FRANK CHURCHILL

Slowly, with feeling

TENOR SAX

BELLA NOTTE

(This Is the Night)

from Walt Disney's LADY AND THE TRAMP

Words and Music by PEGGY LEE
and SONNY BURKE

GIVE A LITTLE WHISTLE

from Walt Disney's PINOCCHIO

7/8

TENOR SAX

Words by NED WASHINGTON
Music by LEIGH HARLINE

HEIGH-HO

The Dwarfs' Marching Song from Walt Disney's SNOW WHITE AND THE SEVEN DWARFS

TENOR SAX

9/10

Words by LARRY MOREY
Music by FRANK CHURCHILL

I'VE GOT NO STRINGS

from Walt Disney's PINOCCHIO

 11/12

TENOR SAX

Words by NED WASHINGTON
Music by LEIGH HARLINE

LITTLE APRIL SHOWER
from Walt Disney's BAMBI

13/14

TENOR SAX

Words by LARRY MOREY
Music by FRANK CHURCHILL

ONCE UPON A DREAM

from Walt Disney's SLEEPING BEAUTY

TENOR SAX

Words and Music by SAMMY FAIN
and JACK LAWRENCE
Adapted from a Theme by Tchaikovsky

Moderately

Orchestra

SOME DAY MY PRINCE WILL COME

from Walt Disney's SNOW WHITE AND THE SEVEN DWARFS

17/18

TENOR SAX

Words by LARRY MOREY
Music by FRANK CHURCHILL

THE UNBIRTHDAY SONG

from Walt Disney's ALICE IN WONDERLAND

TENOR SAX

Words and Music by MACK DAVID,
AL HOFFMAN and JERRY LIVINGSTON

WHEN YOU WISH UPON A STAR

from Walt Disney's PINOCCHIO

21/22

TENOR SAX

Words by NED WASHINGTON
Music by LEIGH HARLINE

Slowly, with feeling

WHISTLE WHILE YOU WORK

from Walt Disney's SNOW WHITE AND THE SEVEN DWARFS

Words by LARRY MOREY
Music by FRANK CHURCHILL

TENOR SAX

WHO'S AFRAID OF THE BIG BAD WOLF?

from Walt Disney's THREE LITTLE PIGS

25/26

TENOR SAX

Words and Music by FRANK CHURCHILL
Additional Lyric by ANN RONELL

YOU CAN FLY! YOU CAN FLY! YOU CAN FLY!

from Walt Disney's PETER PAN

Words by SAMMY CAHN
Music by SAMMY FAIN

27/28

TENOR SAX